You Don't Have To Be Broke

So Wake Up, Shake It Up, And Make a Change!

Joani Ward

You Don't Have To Be Broke
So Wake Up, Shake It Up, And Make A Change!

ISBN 13: 978-0-615-49891-1
ISBN 10: 0615498911

This book is designed to provide an awakening. The stories described in the book are based on true experiences of the Author. The book is sold with the understanding that the Author is not engaged in the business of rendering legal, accounting or other professional services by publishing this book. As each individual situation is unique, questions relevant to personal finances and specific to the individual should be addressed to an appropriate professional to ensure that the situation has been evaluated carefully and accurately. The Author disclaims any liability, loss, or risk which is incurred as a consequence, directly or indirectly, of the use and application of any of the concepts of this book.

Joani Ward is an Assistant Director in the Corporate Financing Department of FINRA, and an Adjunct Professor in the School of Professional Studies at Trinity Washington University. The views discussed herein are solely those of the Author, and do not reflect the views of FINRA or Trinity Washington University.

Printed in the USA by 48HrBooks.com (www.48HrBooks.com)
Cover Design and Artwork: Britlyn Whalum

Dedication

My gratitude and appreciation goes out to many. First, and foremost, the book is dedicated to my Mom and Dad, Zora and William Ward, Sr., for instilling in me the belief that I could accomplish anything.

Second, I take my hat off to Oprah Winfrey for exposing me to a plethora of positivity. Watching Oprah, I became knowledgeable of *The Secret*, Eckhart Tolle and *A New Earth*, Louise Hay and *You Can Heal Your Life*, and numerous others that helped me awaken to a new way of thinking and appreciation for life.

Third, I dedicate my book to Ardyss International. My affiliation, as an Independent Distributor, with Ardyss International introduced me to new and exciting mentors and authors, and helped me develop a millionaire mindset.

Fourth, I thank my mentors, Mr. Tycoon, Coach Janese, and Anthony Morrison for sharing their knowledge and helping me to discover the successes lying dormant within me.

Fifth, to my brothers, William Jr. and Kelvin Sr., thank you for loving me and supporting me through every endeavor.

Last, but not least, my utmost love and appreciation to Ettie Collins and Demetrous Dolberry, my partner and son, for being my sounding boards and support throughout my pursuit to complete my first literary work and to achieve financial independence.

Table of Contents

Acknowledgements

In addition to those identified in my dedication, I'd like to express special thanks to a group of phenomenal individuals. Words cannot describe my appreciation for their confidence and optimism regarding my ability to bring the completion of my book to fruition. I humbly thank each of you for your financial contribution and support.

Elaine Collins
Ellen Collins
Ettie Collins
Rose Hobson
Kemba Walker
Kelvin Ward
Zora Ward
Tanya Wilson

Foreword

I met Joani at a game party I was having on a cold winters Saturday evening, March 22, 2003. Joani seemed quiet and reserved. I knew she was a positive person and someone I would love to have in my circle of friends-well my feeling was correct, as she is and will always be true friends in every sense of the word.

When she asked me to write a foreword on her upcoming endeavor of writing a book, I was flattered. I was even more pleased when she asked me to write it for Chapter 1 – Passion Play.

My passion almost kept me from writing this foreword. I am passionate about life, of course, and TENNIS! When I was asked to focus on writing a foreword about Passion, my thoughts, visions, and mind drifted to the game of TENNIS. OK, I bet you guessed it; my all time passion is tennis.

I started playing tennis back in the 90's, and I've been playing ever since. I play league tennis, World Team Tennis (WTT), recreational tennis, and I officiate matches at every level. I am preparing to make tennis my career. I plan to become an official and a tournament director after completing my first passion job as a teacher.

One passion is taking over another, so I know I should be moving toward my new career in TENNIS.

Since meeting Joani back in 2003, she can see passion play in me when it comes to tennis, and now she's bitten by the Tennis bug.

Welcome to my passion play.

Ellen Collins,
Teacher
Social Worker
Tennis Player

Introduction

I've written this book because I wish I'd been privy to the information I discuss 36 years ago. If I had known the basic concepts of wealth creation when I was 18 years old, I quite possibly would be a billionaire today. What I want to achieve through my book is not only sharing basic concepts, but simplifying the concepts. I also share some of my experiences throughout the book, in hopes that you will find the information more realistic.

I'm a baby boomer, but no matter how young or old you are, you can benefit and apply these concepts to achieve your financial independence, and hopefully avoid the mistakes I have made.

Please understand, I did not create the concepts I discuss; they have been in existence for many, many years. I became knowledgeable of these concepts by reading books, listening to motivational CDs, watching motivational DVDs, and attending seminars and workshops. The works of Napoleon Hill, Robert Kiyosaki, Mark Victor Hansen and Robert G. Allen, George S. Clason, Kevin Trudeau, Zig Ziglar, Myron Golden, David Bach, Mr. Tycoon, and Joseph B. Washington are my inspiration for writing this book.

So, What is Wealth Creation?

In my opinion, wealth creation is the state of making your money work for you, instead of you working for money. Wealth creation is passive income.[1] Wealth creation is working smart, instead of hard. Wealth creation is knowing that an asset isn't really an asset unless it's producing income for you.

Assets vs. Liabilities

You may have a beautiful house and a fancy car, but are these possessions (supposed assets) making you any money? Sure, your house affords certain tax advantages, but on a monthly basis, it's a wealth reducing liability. Also, a new car typically loses 11% of its value the moment you drive it off the lot. During the first five years the car depreciates by 15% - 25% each year, so that after five years, the typical car is worth 37% of what you paid for it at the dealership.[2] Shift your focus to income producing assets, not wealth reducing liabilities. That beautiful house and that fancy car probably take a big chunk out of your monthly earnings, don't they? Be honest.

Additional Streams of Income

What additional streams of income do you have in place to recoup the money you put out for that beautiful house and fancy car?

---

[1] Passive income is earnings an individual derives from a rental property, limited partnership or any other enterprise in which he or she is not actively involved.

[2] http://www.edmonds.com/car-buying/how-fast-does-my-car-lose-value-infographic.html (accessed 6/27/2011)

- Do you have rental properties that are generating income, or are you involved in any other type of real estate transactions that are making money (e.g., tax liens, foreclosures, short sales, or wholesaling)?
- Are you investing in or playing the stock market?
- Are you promoting a company through a CPA or CPL program or acting as a reseller through an affiliate marketing program?
- Involved in multi-level marketing?
- Do you own a business?

If you answered "no" to the questions above, that's alright. It's never too late to start creating wealth. The following chapters describe concepts that separate the haves from the have nots, and should shake you up. An interesting quote by Charles Jones states:

> "You are the same today that you are going to be in five years from now except for two things: the people with whom you associate and the books you read."

Maybe you've heard this quote stated in different ways, but the bottom line is if the people with whom you associate are broke, there's a pretty good chance you'll be broke too. If you want to be wealthy, associate with like-minded people. Surround yourself with positive, successful, wealthy people and learn the secret to their success.

Reading

Reading can change your life. Most knowledgeable people read, while most poor people entertain themselves and spend more time watching television or going to the movies. The books you read can unlock opportunities you have never imagined. Harry S. Truman stated:

"Not all readers are leaders, but all leaders are readers."

This book is a quick read, just enough to wake you up, shake you up, and help you to see that you want to make a financial change in your life. Approach the following chapters with an open mind, and understand that it takes time to create wealth. These concepts are not a get rich scheme. It takes proper planning and focus to create and sustain wealth.

There are many more books I want to read, and more knowledge to acquire, but in the interim I believe it's my duty to share what I've learned with those that are ready to accept and apply the concepts. Going forward, I wish you great wealth and success, and hope that my book adds value to your life.

"To lots of beautiful days and beautiful nights. Welcome to the champagne life. Where trouble is the bubble in the champagne glass, and dreams and reality are one in the same." ~NeYo

Chapter 1 - Passion Play

> "Failure will never overtake me if my determination to succeed is strong enough."
>
> ~Og Mandino

If you are currently employed, I want you to think about your job.[3] Do you wake up every morning excited about the day ahead of you, or do you dread waking up? Are you passionate about the way you spend eight to nine hours of your day? What makes you smile? What makes your heart race? Take a moment and think about your goals, ideas, burning desires, and dreams. Now think about the job you have. Should you be considering a change?

What's Your Dream?

What income producing activity could you do every day, and love, regardless of the amount of time required for the activity? Could it be owning a restaurant? Investing in real estate? Writing books? Creating a new product? I want you to focus on your goals, burning desires, and dreams. As you focus, know that as you shift your thinking, and change your mindset, you will probably come to the realization that you don't like your job. There's something else you'd rather be doing that sets you on fire. I've heard that during your lifetime you will have approximately **three** million dollar ideas per year. Don't

---

[3] Myron Golden defines J.O.B. as an acronym that stands for "Jump Out of Bed", get on the "Journey of Broke", so you can remain "Just Over Broke." Taken from *The Trash Man to the Cash Man.*

overlook them. Pay attention and take action. I paid attention, but I didn't take action.

Million $ Idea #1

Here's a prime example. When I first started working in the financial industry I had an idea to open a deli and name all the food items stock market terms. I discussed my idea with a colleague and he suggested approaching venture capitalists, or an investment banking firm to fund my idea. I pondered over his suggestion and did nothing to bring my idea to fruition.

Several years after having this idea, I was out on my lunch break, and saw an establishment called Wall Street Deli.[4] I couldn't believe my eyes. Wall Street Deli started out as Stand N Snack in 1967, but was  renamed Wall Street Deli in 1987. Along with its new name, the deli underwent a complete redesign that resulted in an upscale, New York style delicatessen serving breakfast specials, sandwiches, wraps, soups and salads. The concept was purchased by WSDS, Inc. in 2002. In 2007 TruFoods, LLC became the franchisor, providing Wall Street Deli with the solid business acumen and strong financial backing the franchise needed to maintain its national presence and continue its growth. Similar to my idea, Wall Street Deli named many of its food items after various areas in New York. For example, some of its specialty sandwiches are named Central Park, Bronx, Brooklyn, Wall Street Club, and Little Italy. This could have been my million dollar baby, but I didn't listen to my colleague's advice.

---

[4] http://www.wallstreetdeli.com (accessed 3/21/2011).

Million $ Idea #2

In addition to the deli idea, I've always had a desire to own a restaurant; something stylish and contemporary. When this idea first surfaced, I was working on my undergraduate degree at George Washington University at Mount Vernon Campus. I didn't have food service or a hospitality background, so after giving the idea some thought, I decided to get a job in a restaurant to learn the business. I worked in the kitchen in a restaurant called the American Café, which was located down the street from Union Station, on Massachusetts Avenue, NE. There was another location in Georgetown, near the corner of M Street and Wisconsin Avenue NW. I loved the American Café for three reasons. One, the wait staff all wore white oxford shirts and khakis – one of my favorite outfits. Two, they made the best chicken tarragon sandwich I had ever tasted. Three, they gave me the opportunity to see what owning and operating a restaurant entailed.

It's a tough business, and it can be stressful. Making sure you have a superior and reliable staff is a key component to maintaining your sanity, and building a successful establishment. If somebody calls in with an unanticipated absence, you, the owner, have to fill in, if you can't contact another employee to fill the slot. Staffing, suppliers, liquor license, employee benefits, insurance, pleasing customers, it's all a lot of stress. Needless to say, after leaving the American Café, I didn't pursue my desire to own a restaurant.

Million $ Idea #3

After receiving my MBA from The Johns Hopkins University (JHU) in May 2001, I attended an Entrepreneur Workshop hosted by JHU. I attended the workshop because I was interested in opening a women's nightclub. I wanted to pattern it after a club I visited in London, sticking with the stylish and contemporary concept. My club needed a special hook[5] to give the two mainstay women's clubs in DC, Phase One and Lace, a lot of competition. I needed something that would lure patrons back for more and more.

JHU engaged bankers, financial planners, investment advisors, successful entrepreneurs, networking specialists, and more to come spend the day with aspiring entrepreneurs. I had a ball, and met lots of great people. My favorite breakout session was with the banker. The banker asked for a volunteer to describe their business venture. Initially, no one spoke up, so I shared my idea. Perfect!! The banker told us he had just financed a Martini Bar in DC, and he took us through all the startup costs and expenses for the bar (see Exhibit 1 – Nightclub Expenses,[6] for an example of the high end and low end expenses). I learned a nightclub is a pricey venture, with a statistically high failure rate. A DC alcohol license alone can run from $1,500 to $4,500, depending on capacity, while a permit costs approximately $3,000. The banker also brought up the

---

[5] A hook is a means of attracting interest or attention; an enticement. http://www.answers.com/topic/hook#ixzz1QD1VxX59 (accessed 4/22/2011)

[6] Fulbright, Jenny, How to Start a Nightclub Business, http://www.powerhomebiz.com/vol141/nightclub2htm (accessed 5/27/2011)

issues of whether to lease or buy a building, and whether to purchase new equipment vs. used equipment. I put this idea on the back burner, but after performing the appropriate financial analysis, and examining the revenue generating metrics, I may seriously reconsider the club being one of the income producing prongs for my new business, Nothing In Between, LLC.

Million $ Idea #4

I love dogs. Fluffy, my first dog, is a West Highland Terrier. She came into my life in April 1999, and changed my life. I was an over-protective pet Mommy, so Fluffy went everywhere with me, or she went to doggie daycare at Best Friends in Gaithersburg, MD. In 2003, three Chihuahua's came into my life along with Ettie and Demetrous; Coco, KK and Ebi. In 2008, I put a picture of three adorable dogs on my vision/dream board,[1] just because they were cute. In 2009, three Jack Russell/Miniature Pincher mix puppies came into my life; Sasha, Bruno and Noah. Since 2009, Asia (a poodle), Oreo (a Jack Russell mix), Bella and Midnight (Asia's puppies) and Cobi (Ebi's puppy) have also come into my life. I told you, I love dogs.

---

[1] A dream board is a visualization tool to help you form a mental picture of your goals and dreams.

Because I know how important pets are to their owners, I had an idea to establish a dog sitting service. My objective was to provide in home care for dogs while there owner(s) was away on vacation, business travel, etc. I felt in home care was important because the dog would be more comfortable in their environment, while the owner was away. My rationale was that this concept would lessen separation anxiety.

I researched what I needed to do to establish my business, and get everything rolling, but somehow I lost momentum. What's my problem? Since 2000, the pet industry has seen a 36% increase in sales, making it a $45 billion per year industry.[8] I'm not taking the appropriate action to bring my ideas to fruition. Why am I leaving money on the table, when it could be in my bank account?

It's All About You

We all have dreams and goals we'd like to accomplish. Don't let those ideas slip through your fingers like I did. Take them seriously, but keep in mind you should LOVE what you do. If you LOVE what you do, you'll be "playing" all the way to the bank. You need a concentrated focus and a burning desire to bring your goals and dreams to fruition. Don't take your ideas lightly. Put your plan on paper. Ask yourself what you need to do, and who you need to talk to accomplish your goal. Create a project chart or some form of time tracker to ensure you are devoting enough time to your goal. I use a project chart

---

[8] Grobin, Joe, Growth of the Pet Industry, Associated Content from Yahoo [http://www.associatedcontent.com/article/111938/growth_of_the_pet_industry.html?cat=9)]. (accessed 4/23/2011.)

provided to me by my mentor, Mr. Tycoon, and an application I purchased for my iPhone called Daily Tracker. Develop a timeline and stick with it.

Also, don't try to take on more than you can handle, or set unrealistic goals for yourself. When I started writing this book I was teaching two classes at Trinity, and working on my internet affiliate marketing business, in addition to working at FINRA from 9:00am – 6:00pm. I was trying to meet an April 30, 2011 deadline for the book, but I was being too ambitious and unrealistic. There were many days that I felt overwhelmed, because I was just trying to do too much. Mr. Tycoon's constant advice and coaching kept me afloat; resulting in the completion of each project I was working on.

As you move forward evaluating your situation, pay close attention to your goals, ideas, dreams and burning desires. If you don't, you may just miss a million dollar opportunity. If you pay attention and follow through with your passions, making your money work for you will be extremely important. Moving into Chapter 2, I discuss the value of money.

Quotes to Live By

"There is no passion to be found playing small – in settling for a life that is less than the one you are capable of living." ~Nelson Mandela

"Great ambition is the passion of a great character. Those endowed with it may perform very good or very bad acts. All depends on the principles which direct them." ~Napoleon Bonaparte

"Live with passion!" ~Tony Robbins

"Passion is energy. Feel the power that comes from focusing on what excites you." ~Oprah Winfrey

Chapter 2 - The Value of Money

> "When I was young, I thought money
> was the most important thing in life.
> Now that I'm old - I know it is."
>
> ~Oscar Wilde

I have been around for 54 years, but just recently read several books that have changed my life regarding wealth creation. The information I learned has altered my whole outlook on money, consumption, and financial independence.

Compound Interest

I receive incentive compensation (a bonus) every year, and have received one for at least the past 18 years. An example of my bonus breakdown is provided in Table 1 (all Appendices, Exhibits, and Tables appear in the back of the book). Table 1 identifies the amount of my yearly bonus (approximations), and the amount of money I took home after taxes and other deductions. During these years I was strictly in consumption mode, requiring instant gratification. After receiving my bonus, I would either hit the mall for a shopping spree, or spend a few hours at a car dealership purchasing a new car.

The aggregate value of the bonuses I received during the 18 year period was $315,325, but after deductions, the bonus payout was reduced to an aggregate of $204,961. There is a term in the business/banking world known as compounding, which refers to earning interest on previous interest.

Table 2 shows how my bonuses could have grown, had I chosen to save them at 6% APY[9] compounded yearly.

With a bonus of $10,000, reduced by 35% due to taxes and other deductions, I hypothetically brought home $6,500. At the end of the year (Dec. 31), I could have hypothetically earned $390 in interest, giving me $6,890 in year 1. In year 2, I brought home a $7,800 bonus. Added to the $6,890 saved in year 1, and factoring in the 6% compounded interest, I could have had $15,571.40 in my bank account, at the end of year 2. Following this same pattern year after year could have resulted in a nest egg of $355,812. Instead, I wanted to buy everything imaginable. Mont Blanc, Rolex, Lexus, Ferragamo, you name it, I had it.

Even if I had put this money under my mattress for the past 18 years, I still would have amassed $204,961. So, what I'm getting at is I didn't make sound financial decisions regarding my bonuses. I didn't save any portion of the bonuses. I spent every penny. I was living within my means, but by not saving anything, I wasn't creating wealth.

The Richest Man of Babylon, *Rich Dad Poor Dad*, and *The Automatic Millionaire* all suggest one foundational concept. That concept is to save 10% of your earnings before you pay anyone else. Whether you put the money in a savings account, brokerage account, 401(k), money market account or under your mattress, is totally at your discretion.

---

[9] Annual Percentage Yield (APY) takes into account compound interest. The APY for a 1% rate of interest compounded monthly would be 12.68% $[(1 + 0.01)^{12} - 1]$. Annual Percentage Rate (APR) does not take into account compounding within the year. If a credit card company charges you 1% interest per month the APR would equal 12% (1% x 12 months).

Seven Rules for Acquiring Money

George S. Clason, author of *The Richest Man of Babylon*, uses short allegorical stories to teach seven simple rules for acquiring money. The rules are as follows:

1. Start thy purse to fattening – set aside ten percent of your wages before any other expenses are handled.

2. Control thy expenditures – plan your expenses wisely and demand value for what you spend.

3. Make thy gold multiply – compound interest, compound interest, compound interest. If you use other investment vehicles to acquire wealth, be cognizant of the risk/reward ratio.

4. Guard thy treasures from loss – if you're going to take investment risks, educate yourself so that you can protect your assets.

5. Make of thy dwelling a profitable investment – own your home instead of renting. If possible, rent a bedroom in the house, therefore creating an income producing asset.

6. Insure a future income – financial safety is key. Additional streams of income, insurance, and a tight savings plan can help to provide financial wellness for you and your loved ones.

7. Increase thy ability to earn – self development, experience, and confidence can improve your income. Your favorite hobby or skill could turn into a million dollar business opportunity.

Discounted Cash Flow Analysis

One of the courses I teach as an Adjunct Professor at Trinity Washington University is Financial Decision Making. The school term commences with me discussing the importance of understanding how to evaluate a company and its performance by interpreting financial statements, such as the Balance Sheet,[10] Income Statement,[11] and Statement of Cash Flows.[12] We also

---

[10] The balance sheet is a financial statement that summarizes a company's assets, liabilities and shareholders' equity at a specific point in time. These three balance sheet segments give investors an idea as to what the company owns and owes, as well as the amount invested by the shareholders. The balance sheet must follow the formula, Assets = Liabilities + Shareholders' Equity

[11] The income statement summarizes a company's revenues (sales) and expenses quarterly and annually for its fiscal year. The final net figure, as well as various others in this statement, is of major interest to the investment community.

[12] The Statement of Cash Flows is one of the quarterly financial reports any publicly traded company is required to disclose to the SEC and the public. The document provides aggregate data regarding all cash inflows a company receives from both its ongoing operations and external investment sources, as well as all cash outflows that pay for business activities and investments during a given quarter.

discuss the importance of understanding financial ratios.[13] The school term ends with me discussing how to value a company by determining it's per share price, using free cash flows, discounted cash flow analysis, and terminal values.

I believe anyone investing their money, be it in the stock market or in business opportunities, should be able to make knowledgeable financial decisions. Having a basic understanding of financial statements and discounted cash flow (DCF) analysis[14] is a definite plus.

Various methods can be used to make financial decisions using DCF analysis. Below is an example of a potential investment opportunity and the DCF techniques used to make the final decision.

An investment costing $40,000 promises an after tax cash flow of $18,000 per year, for 6 years.

---

[13] A financial ratio is the comparison of two numerical values taken from an enterprise's financial statements that help with evaluating the overall financial condition of a corporation or other organization. Financial ratios may be used by managers within a firm, by current and potential shareholders of a firm, and by a firm's creditors.
[14] DCF is a valuation method used to estimate the attractiveness of an investment opportunity. DCF analysis uses future free cash flow projections and discounts them (most often using the weighted average cost of capital) to arrive at a present value, which is used to evaluate the potential for investment. If the value arrived at through DCF analysis is higher than the current cost of the investment, the opportunity may be an acceptable business opportunity.

Accounting Rate of Return

The **Accounting Rate of Return**[15] (ARR) for this investment opportunity is $18,000/$40,000 = 45%. Since our ARR is 45%, it means that the project is expected to earn $0.45 out of each dollar invested. If the ARR is equal to or greater than the required rate of return, the project is acceptable.

Payback Period

Another method that can be used to make financial decisions, but that doesn't consider the time value of money, is the Payback Period.[16] It is calculated as follows: $40,000/$18,000 = 2.2 years to recoup the initial $40,000 investment.

---

[15] The Accounting Rate of Return is a very simple way of estimating a project's net profits, and can provide a basis for comparing several different projects. Under this method of analysis, returns for the project's entire useful life are considered.

$$\text{Accounting Rate of Return} = \frac{\text{Annual Cash Inflows - Depreciation}}{\text{Initial Investment}}$$

[16] The Payback Period is the simplest DCF method, and considers only the period it takes to recoup the original investment.

$$\text{Payback Period} = \frac{\text{Cost of the Project}}{\text{Annual Cash Inflow}}$$

Net Present Value

Net **Present Value**[17] (NPV) can be calculated as follows, using a 15% discount rate:[18]

-$40,000+($18,000 *3.784) = $28,112. The 3.784 represents the present value annuity factor for a 6 year period, with a 15% discount rate. See Appendix B for the present value of an annuity table. If the cash inflows had been different for each year, you would use the values in the present value table in Appendix A for each respective year. Since the NPV result is greater than zero, this can be considered an acceptable business opportunity.

Note: If a value does not appear in Appendix A, for example 8.2%, for period 1, the calculation to determine the present value factor is $1 \div 1.082 = .924214$.

---

[17] Net Present Value is the difference between the present value of cash inflows and the present value of cash outflows.

NPV = -Initial Investment + Cash Inflow(PVAF,r%,n years)

[18] Discount rate refers to the interest rate.

Profitability Index

Still using the 15% discount rate, the **Profitability Index**[19] can be calculated by taking the present value of the cash inflows and dividing by the initial investment: $18,000(3.784)/$40,000 = 1.7. A ratio of 1.0 is logically the lowest acceptable measure on the index. A value lower than 1.0 would indicate that the project's PV is less than the initial investment. As values on the profitability index increase, so does the financial attractiveness of the proposed project.

Internal Rate of Return

Last, but not least is the **Internal Rate of Return**[20] (IRR). This technique is used to measure and compare the profitability of investments. Once you know the rate, you can compare it to the rates you could earn by investing your money in other projects or investments. A business owner will typically insist that in order to be acceptable, a project must earn an IRR that is at least several percentage points higher than the cost of borrowing, to compensate the company for its risk, time and trouble associated with the project. IRR is easily calculated using a financial calculator or Excel. Based on the facts

---

[19] The Profitability Index is an index that attempts to identify the relationship between the costs and benefits of a proposed project through the use of a ratio calculated as:

$$\text{Profitability Index} = \frac{\text{Present Value (PV) of Future Cash Flows}}{\text{Initial Investment}}$$

[20] The internal rate of return on an investment or project is the discount rate that makes the net present value of all cash flows equal to zero.

provided for the sample business situation, the IRR is 39%. (See Appendix C)

The NPV, PI, and IRR indicate that this investment would be acceptable on the basis that the NPV is greater than 0, the PI is greater than 1, and the IRR is greater than the 15% discount rate.

Now, you have a simplified explanation of valuable information to assist with making your money work for you. We discussed compound interest, and a skill set called DCF Analysis. Remember, it's important for you to make educated financial decisions. It's also important that you realize you can't live within your means, but that you should live below your means. If you spend every penny you earn, you will **never** create wealth, because you will never be able to save any money to invest.

Quotes to Live By

"Money, it turned out, was exactly like sex; you thought of nothing else if you didn't have it and thought of other things if you did."~ James Baldwin

"Man was born to be rich, or inevitably to grow rich, through the use of his faculties." ~ Ralph Waldo Emerson

"Wealth comes from knowing what others do not know."
~Aristotle Onasis

"Study well what the billionaire does. It may make you a millionaire." ~ John Emmerling

"Wealth is power. With wealth many things are possible."~ George Clason

Chapter 3 - The Law of Attraction[21]

> "Life can and should be phenomenal...
> and it will be when you unconsciously
> apply the Law of Attraction"
>
> ~Bob Proctor

In January 2006, Oprah Winfrey hosted a segment entitled "Discovering The Secret." I watched in amazement as Rev. Dr. Michael Beckwith, James Arthur Ray, Lisa Nichols and Jack Canfield discussed *The Secret*,[22] how their lives had changed, and the amazing things that can happen in your life if you follow its philosophy. Whether you want wealth, health, a soul mate, or a new job, it's possible if you follow the philosophy of *The Secret*.

The Secret

The creator of *The Secret*, Rhonda Byrne, got her idea when she was suffering physically, emotionally and financially.

---

[21]The Law of Attraction is a metaphysical New Thought belief that "like attracts like," that positive and negative thinking bring about positive and negative physical results, respectively. According to the Law of Attraction, the phrase "I need more money" allows the subject to continue to "need more money." If the subject wants to change this state, they need to focus their thoughts on the goal (having more money) rather than the problem (needing more money).

[22]*The Secret* is a 2006 film produced by Prime Time Productions, consisting of a series of interviews related to the idea of optimistic thinking. It states that everything one wants/needs may be accomplished by wishing it and believing in it. *The Secret* was eventually distributed through DVD, online, and subsequently published as a book.

During this time, Ms. Byrne's daughter gave her a copy of *The Science of Getting Rich.*[23] The information Rhonda uncovered was so powerful that it prompted her to do extensive research, covering a timeframe from 3500 B.C. to the present day.

The Secret refers to the Law of Attraction, or the principle that "like attracts like. The Law of Attraction is a powerful law, and is constantly working. We attract the things we want into our lives, and that is based on what we're thinking and feeling. The principle explains that we create our own circumstances by the choices we make in life. And the choices we make are fueled by our thoughts.

February 2007 Car Accident

According to the Law of Attraction, everything that happens to you—good or bad—you attract to yourself. If this is true, I'm responsible for a February 2007 car accident. I had just returned to DC after visiting my Dad in St. Louis. My Dad had prostate cancer, and his health had deteriorated so rapidly since Christmas, I was extremely worried about him. He was heavy on my mind the morning of the accident. A very pleasant and charming gentleman driving a beautiful CLS Class Mercedes ran a red light at the intersection of 14th Street and Independence Avenue SW around 6:30am. I tagged the back driver side of his car. The gentleman was very polite and apologetic. The police and emergency medical assistance arrived, and the gentleman

---

[23] *The Science of Getting Rich* is a book written by the New Thought Movement writer Wallace D. Wattles. It was published in 1910 by the Elizabeth Towne Company. The book is still in print after 100 years. According to USA Today, the text is "divided into 17 short, straight-to-the-point chapters that explain how to overcome mental barriers, and how creation, not competition, is the hidden key to wealth attraction.

admitted running the red light.   I was taken to George Washington University Hospital for treatment, because my right knee hit the dashboard.   So, did I attract the accident to me because I was more focused on my Dad's condition than on driving?   Were we both worried about pain we were experiencing in our lives, and our pain-bodies[24] caused us to collide? Was I unconsciously worried about having an accident? All good possibilities.

Ask For What You Want

We ask for what we want, either consciously or unconsciously.   It's like making a purchase online.   Whatever you purchase, you expect to receive. That's how the universe is. So if you say, "I don't want to be late," you have really asked to be late. You should have said, 'I am so happy and thankful that I will arrive in divine time. Always turn negative thoughts into positive thoughts.

Everything you focus on can impact your life—books, media, people, thoughts. They all affect how we feel, and the feelings actually send vibrations out into the universe. Anything that's vibrating at a similar level gets attracted into your life.

---

[24] Pain-bodies are negative energy fields that occupy our body and mind. It has two states, active or dormant. When it is active, it is a sign that you are not conscious enough to keep from reacting to the pain in your life. (Pain-bodies is a term described in *A New Earth* by Eckhart Tolle.)

Affirmations

Repeating positive affirmations[25] is a method that can affect and change behavior and habits. This is an effective method for self improvement and for improving one's life, because the subconscious mind accepts and regards repeated thoughts, statements or self-talk as commands. The subconscious mind does not make a distinction between negative and positive thoughts, and treats them both in the same way. Therefore, you must be careful to choose only positive affirmations.

Basic guidelines[26] for repeating affirmations:

1. Phrase your affirmations in the present tense. You want to achieve your goal now, not at some indefinite time in the future. Say, "I have a beautiful new car". Instead of I will buy a new car."
2. Use positive and constructive words to describe your goal.
3. Be specific.
4. Keep affirmations short and easy to remember.
5. Feel and believe that what you are saying is already true.
6. Repeat affirmations at any time of the day. Before falling asleep or upon waking are two excellent times because it's easier to get to the subconscious mind at these times.

---

[25] An affirmation is the practice of positive thinking in New Age terminology.

[26] http://www.successconsciousness.com/affirmations. (accessed 5/29/11)

7. Repeat affirmations aloud, mentally, or by writing them down.

Negativity

Most people focus on negativity. They talk about their current reality. You've heard it —I'm not happy. I feel fat. I'll never find my soul mate. Life's too hard. The economy is never going to recover. I' don't make enough money. I'll never be a millionaire. The more you think and talk about those negative things, the more you attract them. Look at it this way. Your current state is the residual outcome of your past thoughts and feelings. The decisions and choices you made in the past, got you where you are today. So, make a change. Shift your consciousness.

Powerful Thoughts

Thoughts are powerful, but the feelings released from the thoughts are what really attract things into our lives. Many times people are thinking a thought like, "I want to lose 25 pounds," but they look at the scale, see 160 pounds and think, "I'll never lose the weight." On this basis they lose momentum because they feel bad. Instead of all the self-pity, they need to find the positive in the situation. Stop feeling bad about the weight, and instead feel positive that they are willing to do something healthy to improve their situation. Embracing those positive feelings is a key to success.

James Arthur Ray stated:

"In order to attract the things you want into your life—to place the right order—you have to go three for three. Your thoughts, your feelings and your actions all have to be firing simultaneously in the same direction."

Visualization

Visualization helps to direct your thoughts and feelings toward the things you want. You want to be a millionaire? You want to become a famous music producer or a bestselling author? Visualize what you will do when you become a millionaire, famous music producer or bestselling author. Where will you live? Will you travel? Will you own your own business? What will your home look like? What kind of car will you drive? What value will you add, or what kind of difference will you make in someone else's life?

Create a vision board to help you visualize your goals and dreams. My latest vision board appears in Exhibit 1. I created my first vision board during the summer of 2009; the one I mentioned in Chapter 2. You remember, the one I placed the picture of the three adorable puppies on, and a year later acquired three new puppies.

My latest vision board was created in November 2010 at a Dream Maker's Workshop in Atlanta. The workshop was held at the Wealth Factory, and was facilitated by Mr. Tycoon (www.mrtycoon.com) and Coach Janese (www.euphoriccoaching.com). My board identifies some of my dreams and burning desires, which consist of travelling (Great

Pyramids in Egypt, Taj Mahal in India, Ice Hotel in Canada, Ithaa Underwater Restaurant at the Hilton Maldives Resort and Spa), purchasing or building my luxury dream home, buying a Maserati GranTurismo Convertible, having a room in my dream house that has nothing in it but the Bang and Olufsen BeoSound 9000, and a beautifully contoured leather sectional sofa from Roche Bobois, meeting Oprah Winfrey and Eckhart Tolle, owning a successful multi-million dollar company, and winning the PowerBall jackpot. The following words appear at the bottom of my vision board:

"This or Something Better Now Manifests For Me in Divine and Appropriate Timing."

Thoughts and feelings attracting things is an easy concept for most people to put their hands around, but you have to understand some type of action is required to receive the item of desire. You can't watch *The Secret* and think you can visualize receiving an unexpected $50,000 in the next 30 days, and just sit on your butt waiting for the money to appear in your mailbox. You've got to take action. Hence, the Law of Attr**Action**.

According to Jack Canfield, "everything in the world is made up of energy, which is controlled by thoughts and feelings. Thoughts can travel long distances, so you are sending out signals to many people without even knowing it, and these signals attract like energy to you. This means there is no such thing as a coincidence. Everything happens by principles and laws in our universe, so consequently, we have an absolutely unlimited power within us."

An Attitude of Gratitude

The Law of Attraction works best when you have an attitude of gratitude, which shifts your thinking. Be thankful for what you already have, and you open the door to the new things you want in your life. Wake up every morning being thankful. Make a list of everything you're grateful for. Look in the mirror and say "I'm so happy and grateful for a new day, for my loving wife/husband, the roof over my head, the clothing on my back, or whatever you're thankful for." Think of it like this. Your house is full of clutter. You can't receive the new gifts waiting for you until you express gratitude for what you have, and purge the existing items to make room for the new.

This viewpoint applies to all aspects of life. We often focus on what's wrong in our lives. I'm overweight, I don't have enough money. Don't focus on the negative. Appreciate what you have now, accept it, and create an environment where you rejoice in the now, and invite new and better things into your life.

Ask, Believe, Receive

You can start living *The Secret* today by following three simple steps: (1) Ask, (2) Believe, and (3) Receive. Ask for what you want. Write it down. Place your order. Believe that what you've asked for is already yours. Have steadfast faith. Claim it. Ask - I want a successful multi-million dollar business. Believe –The Company I recently launched is a successful multi-million dollar business. Receive – I am so happy and thankful now that my business has generated one million dollars plus in sales.

The action you take has to be from the heart and provide value. What can you give, and how can you serve or add value? When you're in that moment, the universe lines up behind you and it's at your command.

You say you want wealth? Ask for it. Take the action necessary to achieve wealth. Believe in your plan. Attract wealth. Associate with like-minded people. Receive wealth. Remember, if you want the things in your life to change, change the things in your life.

Quotes to Live By

"Take the first step in faith. You don't have to see the whole staircase, just take the first step. ~Dr. Martin Luther King, Jr.

"Thoughts become things. If you see it in your mind, you will hold it in your hand." ~Bob Proctor

"Imagination is everything. It is the preview of life's coming attractions." ~Albert Einstein

"Whatever the mind of man can conceive, it can achieve." ~W. Clement Stone

"When you visualize, then you materialize."~Dr. Denis Waitley

Chapter 4 - Winning Methods

> Accept challenges, so that you may feel the exhilaration of victory.
>
> ~George S. Patton

We're up to Chapter 4, and you're still hanging with me. Excellent!!! Answer a few questions for me. You still want to create wealth? Are you coachable and willing to learn? Willing to change? Do you have a pleasing personality? Do you have good communication skills? These are all elements that, when combined, form winning methods to wealth creation.

There is a story in *The Richest Man in Babylon* that goes something like this:

Algamish,(a wealthy money lender), told Arkad, (eventually the richest man in Babylon), that to become rich you must keep one-tenth of your earnings and don't spend it, no matter what. The earnings will grow, and as the savings accumulate, it will be time to invest, to make the wealth grow. Arkad took Algamish's advice, and started saving one-tenth of his earnings. As the earnings accumulated, Arkad sought the advice of Azmur, a brick-maker, in connection with investing his earnings in jewels. Big mistake, huge!! Ask a brick-maker advice regarding bricks. Ask a jewel merchant advice about jewels. End result, Azmur was cheated and lost all of Arkad's money.

In a movie entitled *The Next Three Days*, starring Russell Crowe and Liam Neeson, a college professor's (John

Brennan) wife (Lara Brennan) is convicted of a murder she says she didn't commit. John plots to break Lara out of prison after multiple appeals are rejected by the judicial system, and Lara attempts to commit suicide. John seeks the advice of ex-convict, Damon Pennington, who successfully staged his own daring prison escape, in order to draw up an airtight plan. John formulates his plan, based on the instruction and advice provided by Damon, and while putting his life on the line, successfully breaks Lara out of prison.

So, based on the two situations I just described, what have you learned? I wanted you to learn the importance of seeking advice from the right people, the experts. Seek advice from someone that has experience, and is successful at what they do. If you want to learn how to invest in real estate, seek out an expert real estate investor. Whatever your passion, if you need guidance, seek out an expert for help. Don't make the mistake that Arkad initially made.

Ardyss International

On October 12, 2009, with a $346 investment, I became an Independent Distributor with Ardyss International. Ardyss International is a multilevel marketing (MLM)[27] business that is geared toward the health and wellness industry. Their products include a line of body reshaping garments that provide instant results (Body Magic), vitamins and drinks which promote health,

---

[27] Multi-level marketing (MLM) is a marketing strategy in which the sales force is compensated not only for sales they personally generate, but also for the sales of others they recruit, creating a downline of distributors and a hierarchy of multiple levels of compensation.

a line of skin care products to promote beauty, and household products.

I listened to a 40-minute telephone call about the company, its products, and the compensation plan. I was hooked. I was excited about the instant gratification the reshaping garments provided, because I had been trying to lose my midsection. The garment helped me lose three sizes in 10 minutes. Really!!! I was a product of the product. The antioxidant drink, LeVive, which was part of the two-step weight reduction program, was delicious and well received by the public. The wealth being acquired by my upline[28] and others was extraordinary.

Be Coachable and Willing to Learn

Two winning methods required in any business are that you need to be coachable and willing to learn. Follow the direction of the people that have already been successful in the business. Follow the leader. In Ardyss, the leaders were making loads of money. Millions!! Dorothy Cook, Helen Dela'Houssaye, and Stormy Wellington, were the leaders that immediately caught my eye. They were beautiful and rich. Since I was new to MLM, I wanted to learn as much as possible. I was like a sponge, because I wanted to make a difference in people's lives while getting paid.

I was definitely coachable and willing to learn. I listened to the 8:00am morning inspiration calls Monday through

---

[28]An upline is a network marketing term for all independent distributors who are above a representative's genealogy, including his or her sponsor.

Friday, attended weekly training/opportunity meetings, listened to the 10:00pm opportunity call every evening so I could perfect my skills of talking about the company, attended weekend training sessions, hosted showcases,[29] talked to numerous people about the company, sent out a mass email campaign introducing my family and friends to Ardyss, attended out-of-town workshops and seminars, created marketing campaigns on Facebook and Google AdWords, placed advertising materials on my car, distributed post cards, participated in numerous vending opportunities, and engaged the Yellow Pages to help me with online marketing. It was all about Ardyss.

Following the advice and instructions of the leaders of Ardyss, I built a team of five people during my first two weeks in the business. Everyone was initially excited about being a part of Ardyss, but I encountered several problems. My organization members had busy lives, so they couldn't find the time to devote to Ardyss. Additionally, everyone on my team was already making good money, and financially comfortable. Many of the Ardyss success stories I heard involved people on the verge of bankruptcy, homelessness, or some extreme need for money, and a corresponding hunger to succeed with Ardyss. My team wasn't driven by that type of hunger.

There was one person in my organization that was actively doing the business. Ettie Collins was the Body Magic and Abdowoman T-Shirt Queen. If her clients didn't have the

---

[29] A showcase is an event where you invite friends and acquaintances to your home or some other location to talk about Ardyss, the products, and the business opportunity. The hook is when you show the transformation; you actually have models from the audience that you put in the reshaping garments. The product sells itself.

$160 for the Body Magic, she would put them on a payment plan, and make sure the money issue didn't result in a lost sale. Brilliant!!! She may have only listened to a few morning inspiration calls, and attended a few training sessions with me, but she had her own way of succeeding.

Staying in step with learning everything possible about the business, I attended a seminar in Atlanta hosted by Helen Dela' Houssaye. One of the speakers was a charismatic, well-dressed gentleman named Mr. Tycoon. He started his presentation by providing some facts about his financial success. Mr. Tycoon has been called one of the toughest real estate negotiators in the South, as well as one of the fairest business men in the industry.

As a former world-class tennis athlete, Mr. Tycoon is no stranger to adversity. After suffering an athletic career ending injury, Mr. Tycoon set his sights on the real estate business. Aggressively dismantling the notion that athletes can't survive without athletics, Mr. Tycoon set the real estate world on fire when he earned over $100,000 in just eight short months of wholesaling. This early success gave him the much needed financial thrust to turn his then home-based business into the thriving corporation of Team Tycoon Inc. This effort has made it one of the most respected and trusted real estate investment firms in Atlanta.

As Founder and Chairman of Team Tycoon Inc., Mr. Tycoon oversees the management of a multi-million dollar real estate investment empire which includes both commercial and residential holdings, educational tools, seminars, private consulting, and personal coaching.

His presentation was filled with statistics regarding what makes you a successful presenter. He talked about what to wear when you're a presenter, how long a person's attention span is, how much information a person retains after a certain number of minutes, and how long you have to make a difference in their life. He also talked about how to formulate your presentation by knowing your audience. Mr. Tycoon captured my undivided attention.

During his presentation he offered a special opportunity to purchase his book entitled *Success is not a Secret It's a System*, attend his Master Presenter's Class, and attend a Dream Maker's Workshop. I couldn't let this opportunity slip through my fingers. I paid my money and anxiously awaited the time to attend the events. I read Mr. Tycoon's book and realized he and Coach Janese were going to be very valuable in my future success. Yes, I met them through my affiliation with Ardyss, but they have taught me so much more than the MLM business.

So, if you want things in your life to change, you have to change things in your life. Be coachable and willing to learn from others who are succeeding at what you want to do. If you are struggling right now, you can't continue doing what you've always done in the past and create wealth. You have got to change. For starters, instead of spending your evening watching your favorite tv show, read a book. I've included a list of suggested readings in the sources section. These books will change your life.

If you have a burning desire to do something, but you don't know how to do it, the Universe will make a way. There's a mentor or an expert to teach you the secret to their success.

You don't need to reinvent the wheel. There are plenty of successful people in the world that can take you under their wing. Take advantage of these opportunities.

Pleasing Personality

It's also important to have a pleasing personality and good communication skills. If you pass someone walking down the street and they smile at you and speak, what do you do? I smile back and speak. A pleasing personality makes you approachable. People are more willing to listen to you if you have a pleasing personality.

Good Communication Skills

Verbal Communications

I also believe good verbal and written communication skills enhance your credibility. I must admit that I had to make an adjustment when I became affiliated with Ardyss. Let me explain. The MLM business doesn't require you to have any level of college education. Therefore, you have people in the business that are financially successful, but that are not very articulate. Their grammar is terrible, but they have a plethora of information to share, that could be vital to your success. Here's an example of something I heard at an Ardyss opportunity meeting. It's not verbatim, but this is the premise of the statement:

"If you are looking to acquire information to help with wealth creation, who are you going to listen to? An educated presenter, who is living paycheck to paycheck saying, "I have a college education" or an MLM presenter, who didn't go any further than high school, but that's averaging $100,000 or more in monthly earnings and saying, "I is a millionaire." If you can get past this issue, the better off you'll be.

Don't get me wrong. I still believe using proper grammar and diction are keys to winning an audience, along with proper presentation preparation driven by audience type, and presentation content.

Written Communications

One of my pet peeves is reading a book or other publication and finding typos and grammatical errors. Nine times out of ten, if I see typos and grammatical errors, I'm not going to finish reading the material. I'm questioning the author's credibility, and whether I should waste my time by continuing to read.

So, please use the tools available to assist with your written endeavors. Use spelling and grammar check, style guides, a dictionary, a thesaurus, and any other sources you deem necessary to ensure the accuracy of your written communication.

Winning Components

Whatever your dreams or desires involve, it's imperative that you follow those that have been successful in your area of interest. Be coachable and willing to learn. Change is good, so be willing to change. Follow a mentor. Follow directions. Talk to **experts** for advice. Be duplicatable. Have a pleasing personality, and **always** use good verbal and written communication skills.

Quotes to Live By

"Failure is success if we learn from it." ~Malcolm Forbes

"You were born to win, but to be a winner, you must plan to win, prepare to win, and expect to win. "~Zig Ziglar

"A person who never made a mistake never tried anything new." ~Albert Einstein

Chapter 5 - The Wealthy You

> Formal education will make you a living; self-education will make you a fortune.
>
> ~Jim Rohn

Wealth Statistics

The following statistics and facts are described in an article entitled *Wealth Statistics: How Do You Measure Up vs. the Average Wealthy American?*[30]

"The average wealthy American has $1,400,000 in assets, and $275,000 in debts, for a net worth[31] of over $1.1 million. Of those assets, they're fairly equally split between "financial" assets (stocks, bonds, mutual funds and cash), and "non-financial assets (real estate, personal business equity, collectibles).

Of the $275,000 in debt, about 80% of it is on properties. (For those of you who still have significant credit card debt, you should know that **the Average Wealthy American has less than 1% of his debt on credit cards**.)

The **usual killers of the middle class – car loans and credit cards** – don't make a dent in the wealthy person's debt load. Wealthy folks generally seem to not live above their means. **Car**

---

[30]Sjuggerud, Dr. Steve, Investment U, [http://www.investmentu.com/2003/January/20030127.html], Monday, January 27, 2003: Issue #208. (accessed 5/15/2011)

[31] Net worth is the grand total of all your assets minus your liabilities.

loans and credit card balances among the wealthy are almost non-existent.

If you're dogged by credit cards and car loans, you may be living beyond your means. Or at the very least, you're not living by the same principles of people who have successfully generated wealth. They don't drive rich. And they don't sit on high interest credit card balances.

The self-employed are the wealthy folks of America. The average net worth of a family where the head of a household works for someone else is $65,000. When it comes to the self-employed, the average net worth is $352,300."

Myron Golden states the following in *From the Trash Man to the Cash Man*:

"of 100 people working from age 20 to age 65, one becomes rich,[32] four become financially independent, five are still working, 28 are dead, and 62 are dead broke."

Statistically, Mr. Golden is making the point that 5% of the people make it financially, and 95% don't. Based on these statistics, it seems logical that if you want to be wealthy, you find out what the people in the 5% bracket are doing, and mirror

---

[32] Are you rich? If you make $250,000 a year, President Obama and Gov. David Paterson of New York think you are. The SEC disagrees. It tells financial firms that a high-net-worth individual is someone with at least $750,000 parked at a particular institution or someone the firm "reasonably believes" to have a net worth exceeding $1.5 million. (Taken from http://money.cnn.com/2009/05/04/news/economy/colvin_rich.fortune/ index.htm) (accessed 7/9/2011)

them. Follow the principles of the rich; not the principles of the poor.

Let me digress for a moment. Did you pay attention to the fact given earlier in this chapter regarding the self-employed being the wealthy people of America?   Look at the numbers. "The **average net worth** of a family where the **head of a household works for someone else** is **$65,000**. When it comes to the **self-employed**, the **average net worth** is **$352,300**." These numbers come from an article that was written in January 2003. The Federal Reserve Board reported the 2007 numbers[33] accordingly; average net worth for head of household working for someone else is $350,000. Self-employed average net worth is $1,961,350.

Self-Employment & Self-Development

If you still want to create wealth, I think you probably agree that self-employment is looking pretty good right about now. What is it going to take for you to become self-employed? Reach back to Chapter 1 – Passion Play. What's your passion? What's your burning desire? What can you provide that will add value to someone? What do global consumers demand?   Do research to determine the products and services that are in greatest demand, have the least competition, and will generate the greatest profit. Self-educate yourself so that you can learn ways to analyze markets, demographics, etc.

I've always been interested in making me the best I can be.   I received my Bachelor's degree from The George

---

[33] http://www.bargaineering.com/articles/average-net-worth-of-an-american-family.html (accessed 5/27/2011)

Washington University – Mount Vernon Campus, and my MBA from The Johns Hopkins University – Carey Business School. Through the years, I've constantly read self-help books, but just recently started to focus on topics in the wealth creation genre. I reflect on the opening quote of Chapter 5,

> "Formal education will make you a living; self-education will make you a fortune."

I believe being self-employed and successful requires a certain level of self-development/self-education. Maybe you're wondering how I define self-development. I like Squidoo's definition.[34] Self development is the set of activities, tasks and study that an individual undertakes as they strive to improve their self knowledge. The aim of self development is to achieve our full potential whether in our professional or personal life.

Self development activities can include, but are not limited to the following:

1. Develop your strengths and talents so that you can achieve your full potential,
2. Fulfill your aspirations and dreams,
3. Become more self aware,
4. Develop work based skills which allow you to increase your income,
5. Help you to develop your spirituality,
6. Enhance your quality of life, and
7. Improve your social skills.

---

[34] http://www.squidoo.com/what-is-self-development (accessed 3/5/2011)

My self development activities include reading every day, listening to motivational cd's, watching motivational dvd's, attending seminars and workshops, taking classes, and working with mentors. During the past 18 months I have read the following books:

1. *Breaking the Spirit of Average*
2. *Success is Not a Secret It's a System*
3. *From the Trash Man to the Cash Man*
4. *Rich Dad Poor Dad*
5. *The One Minute Millionaire*
6. *The Richest Man in Babylon*
7. *Talent is Overrated*
8. *Advertising Profits From Home*
9. *The Hidden Millionaire*
10. *Think and Grow Rich*
11. *The Laws of Success*
12. *The Automatic Millionaire*
13. *Thank You and You're Welcome*

I repeatedly listen to, and watch motivational cd's and dvds. Some include:

1. Kevin Trudeau – *25 Secrets to Wealth Creation,*
2. Mr. Tycoon – *7 Deadly Sins of Real Estate Investing,*
3. Myron Golden – *Bigger, Better, Faster Network Marketing,*
4. Anthony Morrison – *3 Steps to Fast Profits,*
5. Lloyd and Vicki Irving – *How to Build Wealth in the Recession Without Using Your Own Cash or Credit,* and
6. Emmy Vickers – *Raising Your Net Worth Through Networking,*

I've also attended numerous classes, seminars and workshops to develop skills to increase my income.

Nothing In Between, LLC

Most recently, to the tune of $3,600, I took a course through Professional Marketing International (PMI). The reason I took the course was to learn how to setup an affiliate marketing[35] business. The first module of the course requires that you establish your own company, if you intend to engage in affiliate marketing as a reseller. The steps I followed in establishing my company, Nothing In Between, LLC, are as follows:

1. On March 18, 2011 my company was officially formed and registered in Washington, DC through the Articles of Organization.
2. I received my Employee Identification Number[36] on March 21, 2011.
3. On April 20, 2011 I filed the Combined Business Tax Registration[37] Application, and received my Notice of Business Tax Registrations on May 3rd and 9th, respectively.

---

[35] Affiliate marketing is a marketing practice in which a business rewards one or more affiliates for each visitor or customer brought about by the affiliate's own marketing efforts.

[36] An Employer Identification Number (EIN) is also known as a Federal Tax Identification Number, and is used to identify a business entity.

[37] Filing the Combined Business Tax Registration satisfies the initial registration requirement for most DC taxes.

4. I filed my Home Occupancy Permit[38] (HOP) application on May 23rd and it was approved on June 6, 2011.
5. Opened my business bank account on May 26th.
6. Created my initial Cost Per Action (CPA)[39] affiliate marketing website (http://www.mkmoney.info) on May 27th.
7. On June 10th I completed the filing process. I picked up my official HOP, applied for and received my Basic Business License,[40] and picked up a Reseller's Certificate.[41]

There are 8 modules in the PMI Affiliate Marketing Program, which include (1) Business Setup, (2) e-Commerce Basics, (3) Publish Your Website, (4) Essential Site Tools, (5) Link Building, (6) Sponsored Search,[42] (7) Finding Offers, and

---

[38] The Home Occupation Permit (HOP) allows individuals to conduct certain occupations in their principal residences, while at the same time protecting residential neighborhoods from possible adverse effects of those occupations.

[39] Cost Per Action (CPA) is an online advertising pricing model where the advertiser pays for each specified action (a purchase, a form submission, and so on) linked to the advertisement.

[40] In order to operate legally in the District of Columbia, most businesses must get a Basic Business License (BBL) from the Department of Consumer and Regulatory Affairs (DCRA). The Basic Business License (BBL) Program streamlines District of Columbia business licensing procedures. The BBL groups licenses by the type of business activity and regulatory approvals required.

[41] A Reseller Certificate allows you, through your business, to buy goods from your wholesaler (your supplier) without paying tax. It is your responsibility to collect the applicable taxes from your customers when they order the product from you.

[42] When marketing through sponsored search, do not market your CPA website on Google AdWords. You cannot advertise a website in Adwords if the sole purpose of your site is to drive traffic to another site.

(8) Social Media Marketing. Each module includes an interactive lesson, a written guide, and a workbook, if appropriate. I opted to go through the modules and learn the business step-by-step because I want to teach others how to be successful in the online marketing business. If you don't have time to go through the modules, PMI will do all the work for you to the tune of approximately $12,000 (contact and secure your supplier, build your website, and create advertisements for your video marketing campaign).

I've gained a wealth of knowledge since I successfully completed the PMI course, but I have also learned that many people invest in courses like this, but need additional guidance getting everything set up. Your average person is not going to follow the seven steps I just described to establish a business, and complete all the work in the remaining modules.

So, my CPA affiliate marketing website serves two purposes. First, I'm offering instructional guidance and consulting services for others that need help establishing and sustaining their own online businesses, and second, I'm promoting Hostgator, Amazon, and Godaddy on the website. Take action, check out the website.

Quotes to Live By

"It's time we put thoughts of lack behind us. It's time for us to discover the secrets of the stars, to sail to an uncharted land, to open up a new heaven where our spirits can soar."
~Sarah Ban Breathnach

Chapter 6 - Income Producing Assets

> The longer you're not taking action, the more money you're losing.
>
> ~Carrie Wilkerson

In the Introduction, I asked you the following questions:

- Do you have rental properties that are generating income, or are you involved in any other type of real estate transactions that are making you money (e.g., tax liens, foreclosures, short sales, or wholesaling)?
- Are you investing in or playing the stock market?
- Are you promoting a company through a CPA or CPL program or acting as a reseller through an affiliate marketing program?
- Involved in multi-level marketing?
- Do you own a business?

Fundamental Skills Required

As I stated earlier, it's okay if you answered "no" to the questions above. It's never too late to start creating wealth, but you need some fundamental skills under your belt to be successful:

1. Time Value of Money, Discounted Cash Flow Analysis – know how money makes money.
2. Rules and regulations – have an awareness of corporate, state, national and accounting rules and regulations, and comply with them.
3. Watch the market – strategies that worked in 1993 may not work in the current market.

4. Financial finesse - Understand numbers. Know how to evaluate and interpret financial statements, and financial ratios, especially if you are investing in the stock market.

These skills will be invaluable in your pursuit of wealth, regardless the vehicle you use. So, let's get started by talking about affiliate marketing.

Affiliate Marketing

One morning around 3:00am I heard someone on the television describing a way to make money on the internet through affiliate marketing. That someone was Anthony Morrison. Anthony was an entrepreneur from a very young age. When he was 7 years old he asked his Mom if they could get a hot tub like his other friends. His Mom told him if he wanted a hot tub so badly, he should work for the money and buy one. Anthony took heed, went to Sam's Club and bought chocolate bars and sold them door to door. He enlisted the help of his brother and sister with sales, and within three weeks had earned enough money to buy the hot tub.

A year later Anthony overheard a conversation between his mother and father regarding his father's love of the idea of riding a motorcycle with Anthony's uncle on weekends. Anthony went back to Sam's Club and purchased more candy for his campaign to raise money to buy his father a motorcycle. Within a few weeks Anthony had earned $2,000 and purchased his father a Honda Shadow. So, you can see, Anthony was destined to be a successful entrepreneur.

When Anthony's father lost his fortune through an investment in WorldCom stock, Anthony went into action to save the family from total financial ruin. He went into business as an affiliate with an auto parts store, and created his online business, CoolBluePerformance.com. Because he was open 24/7, he stood out from his competitors. He made $4,800 during his first month in business. This is an example of affiliate marketing, and in this instance, the following steps were taken:

1. Anthony acted as a reseller for the auto parts,
2. collected a marked up price for the product,
3. sent the supplier the wholesale cost of the product and the customer order,
4. retained his profit, and
5. the supplier shipped the product to the customer.

There are also more simplified affiliate marketing concepts referred to as Cost Per Lead[43] (CPL) and Cost Per Activity (CPA). CPL advertising typically requires a person to agree to participate in a free trial, by providing their email address. CPA advertising requires the customer to take an action, such as sign up for a service, or make a purchase involving a credit card transaction.

---

[43] Cost Per Lead (CPL) is an online advertising pricing model where the advertiser pays for an explicit sign-up from a consumer interested in the advertiser offer. CPL advertising enables advertisers to generate guaranteed returns on their online advertising dollars, which is especially useful in a tough economy.

Owning Your Own Business

The number one way to reduce your taxes, which helps with wealth creation, is to convert your personal expenditures into allowable deductions. Turn yourself into a business owner. Declare it. Your business doesn't have to make a profit for your expenses to be deductible. All you have to do is establish a "profit motive." [44] Under the Internal Revenue Code, a "profit motive" is presumed if you earn any net income in any three out of five business years. See Appendix H for the business structure for my new business, Nothing In Between, LLC, and Chapter 5 for the steps taken to create the business.

Real Estate Investing

Real estate investing involves the purchase, ownership, management, rental and/or sale of real estate for profit. If you take your time and learn the ropes, you'll discover why real estate is the best wealth builder in the universe. Real estate investments can create multiple income streams and have a river of money flowing your way. Our current economy has turned the real estate market sour for some homeowner's but made the market very attractive for purchasers.

---

[44] A profit motive is the intent to achieve monetary gain in a transaction or material endeavor. Profit motive can also be construed as the underlying reason why a taxpayer or company participates in business activities of any kind. Profit motive must be determined for some transactions to determine the deductibility of any expenses involved.

Bankruptcy Listings

In *Rich Dad Poor Dad*, Robert Kiyosaki described a real estate transaction where he purchased a $100,000 house for $20,000,[45] not from a real estate office, but on the courthouse steps. He borrowed $2,000 from a friend for 90 days, with a promise to repay the initial loan plus $200. Mr. Kiyosaki gave the attorney a $2,000 cashier's check for the down payment. He advertised in the newspaper a $75,000 house being sold for $60,000 with no down payment. Interested purchasers called, and after the house legally belonged to Mr. Kiyosaki, he allowed the interested parties to view the house. The house sold quickly, and Mr. Kiyosaki pocketed $39,800 after repaying his friend's $2,000 loan plus interest, and the $18,000 outstanding balance remaining on the house. $39,800 may seem like a small amount initially, but envision several transactions of this nature, combined with the techniques for money making money, and your wealth will take on a new perspective.

Deadly Sins of Real Estate Investing

I attended a Dream Maker's Workshop in November 2010, which was hosted by Mr. Tycoon and Coach Janese. Before leaving Atlanta I purchased Mr. Tycoon's dvd entitled *Seven Deadly Sins of Real Estate Investing*. Several deadly sins he mentions are:

---

[45] Mr. Kiyosaki sought real estate opportunities that were in bankruptcy proceedings.

1. The blind leading the blind – if you don't know the real estate business, get a mentor that can teach you the ropes.

2. Real estate people are sales people, not investment experts – don't work with a real estate agent. Work with someone knowledgeable in real estate investing. Remember Arkad from Chapter 4?

3. Becoming a real estate investing seminar junkie – you end up spending way too much money on the materials from the seminars, everybody has their own opinion/system, and you're on information overload. Stick with one mentor.

Tax Lien Investing[46]

Another investment vehicle under the real estate umbrella is tax lien investing. State, county and local governments raise money to provide benefits and services via taxation. One type of taxation is a tax on "real property." Pursuant to statute, the owner of a parcel of real property is assessed a dollar amount to pay based on the value of that real property.

This tax is collected by the county where the property is located. If the owner of the property fails to pay the tax, the amount of the tax becomes a lien against the property. A lien against the property does not help the county and local

---

[46] For more details and step-by-step instruction on tax lien investing go to http://www.real-estate-online.com/articles/art-293.html (accessed 3/30/2011)

governments pay the services and benefits they have promised to provide for their citizens.

The county needs the money now, not some time in the future. It needs that money in order to fulfill its budgetary obligations. By state statute, each county is authorized to collect the taxes due that remain unpaid by selling at public auction, either a Tax Lien Certificate or a Tax Deed.

Foreclosures, Wholesaling, and Short Selling

Other considerations for real estate investments are foreclosures,[47] wholesaling,[48] and short selling. [49] Foreclosures can be tricky, and should only be attempted after you have a few years of experience under your belt. Wholesaling is a very low risk way of getting involved in real estate investing, and a way of making quick cash. A snapshot of how wholesaling works is as follows:

---

[47]Foreclosure is the legal process by which a mortgagee, or other lien holder, usually a lender, obtains a termination of the mortgagor's equitable right of redemption, either by court order or operation of law. There are three ways to buy a foreclosure property;.pre-foreclosure, buying at the foreclosure auction, and buying from the lender after the foreclosure sale.
[48] Wholesaling, also known as flipping houses, is the quickest method to make cash in real estate investing. It is also the business model that needs little to no money down.
[49] Short selling involves a mortgage company accepting less than their full payoff in order to get rid of their defaulted loan, prior to having to foreclose on the property.

You are searching for great real estate deals,

1. You find a deal and put the house under contract. When you put a house under contract, you are putting up as little as $10, and ideally no more than $100.[50]

2. You find another investor or retail buyer to purchase the contract to the house from you for a profit above what you agreed to pay the seller.

3. You want to sell the contract quickly.

Short sales are one of the most effective techniques for discounting loans in real estate. One of the most important steps in the short sales process is getting the deed. Beginning investors often skip the step of getting the deed. Getting the deed is important because homeowners often change their minds or want to back out of the transaction. Without the deed they can back out regardless how much work you've put into the transaction. Other important steps[51] include:

1. Contacting the lender to request the short sale packet or workout packet. Don't tell the lender that you are an investor; either tell them you are the buyer or that you are representing the seller,

2. Providing a hardship letter,

---

[50] http://EzineArticles.com/?expert=James_Orr (accessed on 5/30/2011)
[51] www.foreclosureuniversity.com/studycenter/freereports/what_are_sh ortsales.php (accessed 3/18/2011)

3. Provide HUD-1 and Real Estate Purchase and Sales Agreement, and

4. Brokers Price Option (BPO) – A real estate agent will come out and give their opinion on what the house is worth. This is a key component to the short sell process.

If you are new to real estate investing, partner with an expert to learn the ropes. This is a form of the self development I mentioned in Chapter 5. While learning the ropes, you will also be creating wealth.

Stock Market

I starting working at FINRA[52] (fka National Association of Securities Dealers or NASD) in 1983, and became fascinated with the stock market. I got my first real taste of the stock market when I worked as a Historical Information Specialist. I researched stocks traded on Nasdaq[53] for customers, regulators, and other departments within the Association. I subsequently worked as an Analyst in the Corporate Financing Department, and reviewed and regulated offerings for companies that wanted to sell their stock to the public. Last, but not least, I worked in Nasdaq Listing Qualifications, where I was responsible for overseeing approximately 100+ companies, and ensuring that they continued to meet the requirements for listing on Nasdaq.

---

[52] The Financial Industry Regulatory Authority is a private corporation that acts as a self-regulatory organization (SRO). FINRA performs financial regulation of member brokerage firms and exchange markets.
[53] Nasdaq is the largest electronic screen-based equity securities trading market in the United States and second largest by market capitalization in the world.

Investing in the stock market can be an excellent vehicle to wealth creation, but it does involve risk. The greater the risk, typically, the higher the return potential. Remember the dot-com bubble?[54] The stock market was flying high from 1995 to 2000, with a climax on March 10, 2000; Nasdaq peaked at 5132.52. In 1999, there were 457 IPOs[55], most of which were internet and technology related. Of those 457 IPOs, 117 doubled in price on their first day of trading.[56] People made a lot of money. Then the market crashed, and people lost a lot of money.

If you are very risk averse, the investments paying the highest returns might not be the answer for you. Maybe bonds[57] suit you better. It all depends on your objective for investing in the stock market. Is it for long-term growth, or do you want to make a quick buck? There are numerous products and investment vehicles to choose from, such as common stock, preferred stock, commodities, derivatives, futures, options, Real Estate Investment Trusts (REITs), penny stocks, partnerships, trading on margin, doing a short sale, and on and on. The opportunities are endless.

---

[54] The dot-com bubble was a speculative bubble during which stock markets in industrialized nations saw their equity value rise rapidly from growth in the internet sector and related fields. The period was marked by the founding of a group of new internet-based companies commonly referred to as dot-coms.

[55] IPO – An initial public offering is when a company (called an issuer) issues common stock or shares to the public for the first time.

[56] http://worldeconomiccrisis.blogspot.com/2007/12/2000-dot-com-crash-2000-mar-11-to-2002.html (accessed 5/24/2011)

[57] A bond is a type of debt security that requires an initial investment, usually $1,000, and has an associated interest component (coupon) that is payable to the investor yearly or bi-yearly. The initial investment is repaid upon maturity of the bond.

If you want to invest in the stock market you need to establish an account with a full service brokerage or a discount brokerage. The type of brokerage you select should be determined by your level of investing experience. Don't make investment decisions haphazardly. Be an educated investor. Review registration statements[58]/offering circulars,[59] financial statements, 10-Ks,[60] 10-Qs,[61] and 8-Ks.[62]

Network Marketing/Multi-Level Marketing (MLM)

My initial encounter with Ardyss International, an MLM company, is described in Chapter 4. I changed a lot through my association with Ardyss. I desperately wanted to be successful and make lots of money doing the business. I was an introvert, and didn't like networking. In order to be successful in this type business you can't be shy. You have to talk to people, let them

---

[58] In the United States, a registration statement is a set of documents, including a prospectus, that a company must file with the U.S. Securities and Exchange Commission (SEC) before it proceeds with a public offering. The documents disclose pertinent information about the offering, such as type of securities being offered to the public, offering price, FINRA members participating in the distribution, use of proceeds, existing shareholders, and tax consequences.
[59] An offering circular allows investors to access information regarding a new issue. It provides them with the important highlights without having them actually read the long-form prospectus.
[60] A Form 10-K is an annual report required by the SEC that gives a comprehensive summary of a public company's performance.
[61] A Form 10-Q is a quarterly report filed with the SEC and designed to give a status of how a business is doing after three months of operation.
[62] A Form 8-K is used to notify investors of any unscheduled material event that is important to shareholders or the SEC. After a significant event like bankruptcy or departure of a CEO, a public company generally must file a Current Report on Form 8-K with the SEC within four business days to provide an update to previously filed quarterly reports or annual reports.

know who you are, tell them about your product or service. Make them remember you.

I attended networking events, and often felt very intimidated. Can you imagine a new network marketer walking alone into a room filled with approximately 250 people? I was excited with the potential of the number of contacts I could make, and scared to the point of wanting to turn around and walk out the door. The upside is that I met a very nice couple that gave me networking advice, and helped me to relax. On the downside, I encountered a woman at a different networking event who had recently lost her job. As I introduced myself, I talked about one of my products, the Body Magic Reshaping Garment. This is how I always introduced myself. The woman was obese, and immediately cut me off, telling me she didn't need anything like the Body Magic. Well, I wasn't trying to sell her the garment; just introducing myself and my company. In MLM terms, this lady was a rotten apple.[63] I was a little disheartened by her behavior, but I shook it off.

There are all types of tips and tricks for being successful in an MLM, and various ways to identify the people you should bring into your organization (downline[64]). Everyone is not qualified to do network marketing, but with the right people in your downline, an MLM can be a very lucrative business. It's an exciting industry if you are able to build your network with duplicatable people.

---

[63] A rotten apple is someone that has a negative attitude toward the company, products, etc.

[64] A downline consists of the distributors under you and a hierarchy of multiple levels of compensation.

As of December 31, 2010, the top 10[65] MLMs are:

1. Amway
2. Herbalife
3. CAN
4. Pre-Paid Legal
5. USANA
6. Nu Skin
7. Forever Living
8. Arbonne
9. 4Life
10. Advocare

Ardyss International ranks 49 out of 655 home-based businesses actively tracked in www.mlmrankings.com.

Other Income Producing Assets

As I close this chapter, let me mention a few other income producing assets. Myron Golden and Robert Kiyosaki introduced me to a whole new world when I read their books. They both talked about investments that require little work, if any, on your part, but produce income. I'm referring to things like parking lots, laundromats, car washes, and vending machines. These types of assets are money makers, and don't require a lot of people to run the operation.

With modern technology, parking lots can be totally automated. There are a number of locations in the DC metropolitan area that utilize automated parking facilities. Prime

---

[65] www.nexera.com/top25. (accessed 4/15/2011)

locations are Washington National Harbor, Regan National and BWI airports, and the Department of Consumer and Regulatory Affairs.

It typically takes one or two people to be onsite at a laundromat. A consideration might also be to offer laundry service to your customers (wash, dry and fold) and charge by the pound. While this may be a little costly for some people, busy folks like me love this service.

Approximately 9 people are needed to perform the tasks at a car wash. You need someone to take the customer order, two people to vacuum the inside of the car and scrub the tires, a cashier, and four to five people to wipe down the car. Do you need to retain an onsite mechanic to reduce downtime? Maybe, maybe not.

For vending machines, you would need a computerized system for monitoring inventory, and one or two people to keep the machines stocked; that's if you don't want to restock yourself. I was interested in a vending machine franchise with  Fresh Healthy Vending. Their whole concept is in line with Michelle Obama's vision of healthier eating for school children. This investment opportunity required $120,000 to get started with 10 vending machines, and an assigned territory. Why didn't I take advantage of the opportunity? First, I wasn't able to get enough information from company representatives to perform a discounted cash flow analysis. Remember, it's very important to make educated financial decisions regarding business investments. And second, the company only wanted liquid investors. My funding would have come from a loan through the Small Business Administration, or other lending facility, so I had to forego this opportunity.

With a key location for each of the income producing assets mentioned, you could have an MBA-Massive Bank Account. Keep them in mind as you move forward with your plan for wealth creation.

Quotes to Live By

"Most great people have attained their greatest success just one step beyond their greatest failure." ~Napoleon Hill

"He who begins many things finishes but few." ~German Proverb

"Keep away from people who try to belittle your ambitions. Small people always do that, but the really great make you feel that you, too, can become great." ~Mark Twain

Chapter 7 - Now, What Are You Going To Do?

> "All changes, even the most longed for, have their melancholy; for what we leave behind us is a part of ourselves; we must die to one life before we can enter another."
>
> ~Anatole France

You made it to the end of the book. Congratulations!! Now, are you going to wake up, shake it up, and make a change toward achieving your financial freedom? Or will you continue to do the same old things you've consistently done? I'm hoping you chose option #1.

We covered a lot of ground in the prior six chapters. I shared some of my experiences, and presented facts and concepts that have been utilized by the wealthy for years. Let's review.

We talked about passions, dreams and burning desires in Chapter 1 and how paying attention and taking action could result in a very lucrative business opportunity.

"Nothing great in the world has ever been accomplished without passion." ~Georg Wilhelm Friedrich Hegel

It's absolutely necessary to have a definite goal, and place all your energy, willpower and effort into achieving your goal. Create a plan, and burn all bridges behind you, so you can't retreat. If its riches you desire, Napoleon Hill, the author of *Think and Grow Rich*, describes six definite steps that should be taken:

1. Fix in your mind the exact amount of money you desire.
2. Determine what you intend to give for the money you desire.
3. Establish a definite date when you intend to possess the money you desire.
4. Create a definite plan for carrying out your desire, and begin at once, ready or not, to put the plan into action.
5. Write out a clear, concise statement of the amount of money you intend to acquire. Name the time limit for its acquisition. State what you intend to give in return for the money, and describe clearly the plan through which you intend to accumulate it.
6. Read your written statement aloud, twice daily, once after rising in the morning, and just before retiring at night. See, feel and believe you are in possession of the money.

In Chapter 2 we discussed the time value of money; compound interest, rules for acquiring money, and discounted cash flow techniques used to make financial decisions.

"Part of your heritage in this society is the opportunity to become financially independent." ~Jim Rohn

As you go forward with your plan to create wealth, remember (1) to pay yourself before you pay anyone else, and (2) make educated financial decisions.

We covered the Law of Attraction in Chapter 3. What you think about, you bring about. Chapter 4 focused on the winning methods required for success, and Chapter 5 dealt with the self-development required to achieve your fortune. Last, but not least, Chapter 6 delved into the subject of income producing assets.

I hope the material I've included in this book will make a profound difference in your life. If I've added any value, then my mission is complete. Share this information with your children, spouses, parents and friends, and make a difference in their lives. As you make changes in your life, I'd love to hear about your successes. Please visit my website at www.nothinginbetweenllc.com and share your story.

Keep the following in mind with respect to managing your money as you create wealth.[66]

"We are to be wise with our money. We are to save money, but not hoard it. We are to spend money, but with discretion and control. We are to give back to the Lord, joyfully and sacrificially. We are to use our money to help others, but with discernment and the guidance of God's Spirit. It is not wrong to be rich, but it is wrong to love money. It is not wrong to be poor, but it is wrong to waste money on trivial things. The Bible's consistent message on managing money is to be wise."

Peace and Blessings.

---

[66] http://www.ehow.com/about_4572010_what-does-bible-say-wealth.html#ixzz1GnCcDpyp. (accessed 3/15/11)

About the Author

Joani Ward was born in St. Louis, MO and moved to Washington, DC in 1975 to attend Howard University. She left Howard University and later received her Bachelor's Degree from The George Washington University at Mount Vernon Campus. Joani subsequently received her MBA, concentration in Corporate Finance, from The Johns Hopkins University, Carey School of Business, in May 2001.

This is Joani's first literary work, but rest assured, it won't be her last. She is following in the footsteps of great authors like Jack Canfield and Mark Victor Hansen, Robert Kiyosaki, David Bach, George S. Clason, and Napoleon Hill.

Sources

(Bibliography/Recommended Reading)

Bach, David, December 27, 2005, <u>The Automatic Millionaire.</u> Broadway Books

Bandler, James, 1994, <u>How To Use Financial Statements: A Guide to Understanding The Numbers.</u> McGraw-Hill

Byrne, Rhonda, 2006, <u>The Secret.</u> New York, NY and Hillsboro, Oregon: Atria Books/Beyond Words

Clason, George S., February 3, 2004, <u>The Richest Man in Babylon.</u> Signet.

Colvin, Geoff, May 25, 2010, <u>Talent is Overrated.</u> Portfolio Trade

Golden, Myron, <u>From The Trash Man To The Cash Man.</u> Myron Golden Enterprises.

Hansen, Mark Victor and Allen, Robert G., August 4, 2009, <u>The One Minute Millionaire.</u> Three Rivers Press

Higgins, Robert C., 2009, <u>Analysis For Financial Management.</u> McGraw-Hill

Hill, Napoleon, October 2, 2008, <u>Think and Grow Rich.</u> Strand, London: Penguin Group

Hill, Napoleon, 2006, <u>The Law of Success.</u> Beverly, Massachusetts; Orne Publishing

Kiyosaki, Richard, and Lechter, Sharon L., April 7, 2009, <u>Rich Dad Poor Dad.</u> Running Press Miniature Editions

Morris, Virginia B. and Morris, Kenneth M., 2000, <u>Dictionary of Financial Terms</u>. New York, NY, Lightbulb Press

Morrison, Anthony, 2009, <u>Advertising Profits From Home.</u> Visionary Strategies

Morrison, Anthony, September 1, 2008, <u>The Hidden Millionaire: Twelve Principles to Uncovering the Entrepreneur in You.</u> Morrison Publishing

Mr. Tycoon, Gaines, Eulette, and Holliman, Ron, December 1, 2007, <u>Success Is Not A Secret It's A System.</u> Atlanta, GA: Team Tycoon.

Washington, Joseph B., 2006, <u>Breaking the Spirit of Average.</u>

West, Kanye, March 1, 2009, <u>Thank You and You're Welcome.</u> Super Good LLC

Quotes

http://thinkexist.com/quotations/

http://www.famousquotesandauthors.com/topics/

http://ezinearticles.com/?Top-40-Wealth-Quotations&id=438311

http://www.woopidoo.com/business_quotes/

Present Value Tables

http://www.swlearning.com/finance/brigham/ffm10e/pvtables.html

Financial Ratios

http://mba-accounting.a-z-finance.net/financial-ratio-table

Table 1 – Bonuses without Compound Interest

Year	Bonus Amount	% Withheld (Taxes, etc.)	Remainder
1	$10,000	0.35	$6,500.00
2	$12,000	0.35	$7,800.00
3	$14,000	0.35	$9,100.00
4	$16,000	0.35	$10,400.00
5	$16,800	0.35	$10,920.00
6	$17,000	0.35	$11,050.00
7	$17,200	0.35	$11,180.00
8	$17,500	0.35	$11,375.00
9	$17,825	0.35	$11,586.25
10	$18,000	0.35	$11,700.00
11	$19,000	0.35	$12,350.00
12	$20,000	0.35	$13,000.00
13	$20,000	0.35	$13,000.00
14	$20,000	0.35	$13,000.00
15	$20,000	0.35	$13,000.00
16	$20,000	0.35	$13,000.00
17	$20,000	0.35	$13,000.00
18	$20,000	0.35	$13,000.00
Totals	$315,325		$204,961.25

Table 2 – Bonuses with Compound Interest

Year	Bonus After Deductions	Bonus Invested at 6% APY
1	$6,500.00	6,890.00
2	$7,800.00	15,571.40
3	$9,100.00	26,151.68
4	$10,400.00	38,744.79
5	$10,920.00	52,644.67
6	$11,050.00	67,516.35
7	$11,180.00	83,418.13
8	$11,375.00	100,480.72
9	$11,586.25	118,790.99
10	$11,700.00	138,320.45
11	$12,350.00	159,710.68
12	$13,000.00	183,073.32
13	$13,000.00	207,837.72
14	$13,000.00	234,087.98
15	$13,000.00	261,913.26
16	$13,000.00	291,408.05
17	$13,000.00	322,672.54
18	$13,000.00	355,812.89

Exhibit 1 – Nightclub Expenses

Type of Expense	Low-End Estimate	High-End Estimate
Rent (security deposit & first month)	$3,000	$12,000
Leasehold improvements (heating/air conditioning, electrical, plumbing, painting, carpentry, kitchen upgrade, restroom upgrade, flooring, smoke detectors)	$25,000	$150,000
Interior Design and Refurbishing (including tables, chairs)	$15,000	$45,000
Equipment/Fixtures (audio/lighting lease payment, DJ sound system, bar equipment, lasers, smoke machines, stage sets, mirror objects, other equipment)	$35,000	$125,000
Kitchen Equipment (draft dispenser, microbrew equipment, commercial kitchen, hand sinks, concession equipment, etc.)	$10,000	$40,000
Cash Reserves	$50,000	$150,000
Signage (exterior, exit signs, etc.)	$5,000	$15,000
Legal Fees, Licenses and Permits	$18,000	$40,000
Point of Sales systems (including merchant accounts, credit card terminals, etc.)	$10,000	$35,000
Fire Fighting Enterprises (fire sprinkler systems, fire alarm, fire extinguishers, etc.)	$15,000	$30,000
Beginning Inventory (bar supplies, food)	$15,000	$40,000
Opening Salaries Deposits	$15,000	$50,000
Insurance	$500	$4,000
Grand Opening Marketing	$1,000	$25,000
Other Expenses	Add 10% of total	Add 10% of total
TOTAL START-UP EXPENSE	$239,250	$837,100

Exhibit 2 - Vision Board

Appendix A – Present Value Table

Present value interest factor of $1 per period at i% for n periods, PVIF(i,n).

Period	1%	2%	3%	4%	5%	6%	7%	8%	9%	10%	11%	12%	13%	14%	15%	16%	17%	18%	19%	20%
1	0.990	0.980	0.971	0.962	0.952	0.943	0.935	0.926	0.917	0.909	0.901	0.893	0.885	0.877	0.870	0.862	0.855	0.847	0.840	0.833
2	0.980	0.961	0.943	0.925	0.907	0.890	0.873	0.857	0.842	0.826	0.812	0.797	0.783	0.769	0.756	0.743	0.731	0.718	0.706	0.694
3	0.971	0.942	0.915	0.889	0.864	0.840	0.816	0.794	0.772	0.751	0.731	0.712	0.693	0.675	0.658	0.641	0.624	0.609	0.593	0.579
4	0.961	0.924	0.888	0.855	0.823	0.792	0.763	0.735	0.708	0.683	0.659	0.636	0.613	0.592	0.572	0.552	0.534	0.516	0.499	0.482
5	0.951	0.906	0.863	0.822	0.784	0.747	0.713	0.681	0.650	0.621	0.593	0.567	0.543	0.519	0.497	0.476	0.456	0.437	0.419	0.402
6	0.942	0.888	0.837	0.790	0.746	0.705	0.666	0.630	0.596	0.564	0.535	0.507	0.480	0.456	0.432	0.410	0.390	0.370	0.352	0.335
7	0.933	0.871	0.813	0.760	0.711	0.665	0.623	0.583	0.547	0.513	0.482	0.452	0.425	0.400	0.376	0.354	0.333	0.314	0.296	0.279
8	0.923	0.853	0.789	0.731	0.677	0.627	0.582	0.540	0.502	0.467	0.434	0.404	0.376	0.351	0.327	0.305	0.285	0.266	0.249	0.233
9	0.914	0.837	0.766	0.703	0.645	0.592	0.544	0.500	0.460	0.424	0.391	0.361	0.333	0.308	0.284	0.263	0.243	0.225	0.209	0.194
10	0.905	0.820	0.744	0.676	0.614	0.558	0.508	0.463	0.422	0.386	0.352	0.322	0.295	0.270	0.247	0.227	0.208	0.191	0.176	0.162
11	0.896	0.804	0.722	0.650	0.585	0.527	0.475	0.429	0.388	0.350	0.317	0.287	0.261	0.237	0.215	0.195	0.178	0.162	0.148	0.135
12	0.887	0.788	0.701	0.625	0.557	0.497	0.444	0.397	0.356	0.319	0.286	0.257	0.231	0.208	0.187	0.168	0.152	0.137	0.124	0.112
13	0.879	0.773	0.681	0.601	0.530	0.469	0.415	0.368	0.326	0.290	0.258	0.229	0.204	0.182	0.163	0.145	0.130	0.116	0.104	0.093
14	0.870	0.758	0.661	0.577	0.505	0.442	0.388	0.340	0.299	0.263	0.232	0.205	0.181	0.160	0.141	0.125	0.111	0.099	0.088	0.078
15	0.861	0.743	0.642	0.555	0.481	0.417	0.362	0.315	0.275	0.239	0.209	0.183	0.160	0.140	0.123	0.108	0.095	0.084	0.074	0.065
16	0.853	0.728	0.623	0.534	0.458	0.394	0.339	0.292	0.252	0.218	0.188	0.163	0.141	0.123	0.107	0.093	0.081	0.071	0.062	0.054
17	0.844	0.714	0.605	0.513	0.436	0.371	0.317	0.270	0.231	0.198	0.170	0.146	0.125	0.108	0.093	0.080	0.069	0.060	0.052	0.045
18	0.836	0.700	0.587	0.494	0.416	0.350	0.296	0.250	0.212	0.180	0.153	0.130	0.111	0.095	0.081	0.069	0.059	0.051	0.044	0.038
19	0.828	0.686	0.570	0.475	0.396	0.331	0.277	0.232	0.194	0.164	0.138	0.116	0.098	0.083	0.070	0.060	0.051	0.043	0.037	0.031
20	0.820	0.673	0.554	0.456	0.377	0.312	0.258	0.215	0.178	0.149	0.124	0.104	0.087	0.073	0.061	0.051	0.043	0.037	0.031	0.026
25	0.780	0.610	0.478	0.375	0.295	0.233	0.184	0.146	0.116	0.092	0.074	0.059	0.047	0.038	0.030	0.024	0.020	0.016	0.013	0.010
30	0.742	0.552	0.412	0.308	0.231	0.174	0.131	0.099	0.075	0.057	0.044	0.033	0.026	0.020	0.015	0.012	0.009	0.007	0.005	0.004
35	0.706	0.500	0.355	0.253	0.181	0.130	0.094	0.068	0.049	0.036	0.026	0.019	0.014	0.010	0.008	0.006	0.004	0.003	0.002	0.002
40	0.672	0.453	0.307	0.208	0.142	0.097	0.067	0.046	0.032	0.022	0.015	0.011	0.008	0.005	0.004	0.003	0.002	0.001	0.001	0.001
50	0.608	0.372	0.228	0.141	0.087	0.054	0.034	0.021	0.013	0.009	0.005	0.003	0.002	0.001	0.001	0.001	0.000	0.000	0.000	0.000

Appendix B – Present Value Annuity Table

Present value interest factor of an (ordinary) annuity of $1 per period at i% for n periods, PVIFA(i,n).

Period	1%	2%	3%	4%	5%	6%	7%	8%	9%	10%	11%	12%	13%	14%	15%	16%	17%	18%	19%	20%
1	0.990	0.980	0.971	0.962	0.952	0.943	0.935	0.926	0.917	0.909	0.901	0.893	0.885	0.877	0.870	0.862	0.855	0.847	0.840	0.833
2	1.970	1.942	1.913	1.886	1.859	1.833	1.808	1.783	1.759	1.736	1.713	1.690	1.668	1.647	1.626	1.605	1.585	1.566	1.547	1.528
3	2.941	2.884	2.829	2.775	2.723	2.673	2.624	2.577	2.531	2.487	2.444	2.402	2.361	2.322	2.283	2.246	2.210	2.174	2.140	2.106
4	3.902	3.808	3.717	3.630	3.546	3.465	3.387	3.312	3.240	3.170	3.102	3.037	2.974	2.914	2.855	2.798	2.743	2.690	2.639	2.589
5	4.853	4.713	4.580	4.452	4.329	4.212	4.100	3.993	3.890	3.791	3.696	3.605	3.517	3.433	3.352	3.274	3.199	3.127	3.058	2.991
6	5.795	5.601	5.417	5.242	5.076	4.917	4.767	4.623	4.486	4.355	4.231	4.111	3.998	3.889	3.784	3.685	3.589	3.498	3.410	3.326
7	6.728	6.472	6.230	6.002	5.786	5.582	5.389	5.206	5.033	4.868	4.712	4.564	4.423	4.288	4.160	4.039	3.922	3.812	3.706	3.605
8	7.652	7.325	7.020	6.733	6.463	6.210	5.971	5.747	5.535	5.335	5.146	4.968	4.799	4.639	4.487	4.344	4.207	4.078	3.954	3.837
9	8.566	8.162	7.786	7.435	7.108	6.802	6.515	6.247	5.995	5.759	5.537	5.328	5.132	4.946	4.772	4.607	4.451	4.303	4.163	4.031
10	9.471	8.983	8.530	8.111	7.722	7.360	7.024	6.710	6.418	6.145	5.889	5.650	5.426	5.216	5.019	4.833	4.659	4.494	4.339	4.192
11	10.368	9.787	9.253	8.760	8.306	7.887	7.499	7.139	6.805	6.495	6.207	5.938	5.687	5.453	5.234	5.029	4.836	4.656	4.486	4.327
12	11.255	10.575	9.954	9.385	8.863	8.384	7.943	7.536	7.161	6.814	6.492	6.194	5.918	5.660	5.421	5.197	4.988	4.793	4.611	4.439
13	12.134	11.348	10.635	9.986	9.394	8.853	8.358	7.904	7.487	7.103	6.750	6.424	6.122	5.842	5.583	5.342	5.118	4.910	4.715	4.533
14	13.004	12.106	11.296	10.563	9.899	9.295	8.745	8.244	7.786	7.367	6.982	6.628	6.302	6.002	5.724	5.468	5.229	5.008	4.802	4.611
15	13.865	12.849	11.938	11.118	10.380	9.712	9.108	8.559	8.061	7.606	7.191	6.811	6.462	6.142	5.847	5.575	5.324	5.092	4.876	4.675
16	14.718	13.578	12.561	11.652	10.838	10.106	9.447	8.851	8.313	7.824	7.379	6.974	6.604	6.265	5.954	5.668	5.405	5.162	4.938	4.730
17	15.562	14.292	13.166	12.166	11.274	10.477	9.763	9.122	8.544	8.022	7.549	7.120	6.729	6.373	6.047	5.749	5.475	5.222	4.990	4.775
18	16.398	14.992	13.754	12.659	11.690	10.828	10.059	9.372	8.756	8.201	7.702	7.250	6.840	6.467	6.128	5.818	5.534	5.273	5.033	4.812
19	17.226	15.678	14.324	13.134	12.085	11.158	10.336	9.604	8.950	8.365	7.839	7.366	6.938	6.550	6.198	5.877	5.584	5.316	5.070	4.843
20	18.046	16.351	14.877	13.590	12.462	11.470	10.594	9.818	9.129	8.514	7.963	7.469	7.025	6.623	6.259	5.929	5.628	5.353	5.101	4.870
25	22.023	19.523	17.413	15.622	14.094	12.783	11.654	10.675	9.823	9.077	8.422	7.843	7.330	6.873	6.464	6.097	5.766	5.467	5.195	4.948
30	25.808	22.396	19.600	17.292	15.372	13.765	12.409	11.258	10.274	9.427	8.694	8.055	7.496	7.003	6.566	6.177	5.829	5.517	5.235	4.979
35	29.409	24.999	21.487	18.665	16.374	14.498	12.948	11.655	10.567	9.644	8.855	8.176	7.586	7.070	6.617	6.215	5.858	5.539	5.251	4.997
40	32.835	27.355	23.115	19.793	17.159	15.046	13.332	11.925	10.757	9.779	8.951	8.244	7.634	7.105	6.642	6.233	5.871	5.548	5.258	4.997
50	39.196	31.424	25.730	21.482	18.256	15.762	13.801	12.233	10.962	9.915	9.042	8.304	7.675	7.133	6.661	6.246	5.880	5.554	5.262	4.999

Appendix C – Excel Calculations for DCF Analysis

Rate	15%			
Outflow	-40,000			
Inflow Yr 1	18000			
Inflow Yr 2	18000			
Inflow Yr 3	18000			
Inflow Yr 4	18000			
Inflow Yr 5	18000			
Inflow Yr 6	18000			
NPV	$28,120.69	Formula = NPV(B1,B3:B8)+B2		
Payback	2.2	Formula = Outflow/Inflow		
ARR	0.45	Formula = Inflow/Outflow		
PI	1.7	Formula = PV of Inflows/Outflow		
IRR	39%	Formula = IRR(B2:B8)		

Appendix D - Balance Sheet

ASSETS		LIABILITIES	
Current Assets		**Current Liabilities**	
Cash	$ 2,100	Notes Payable	$ 5,000
Petty Cash	100	Accounts Payable	35,900
Temporary Investments	10,000	Wages Payable	8,500
Accounts Receivable - net	40,500	Interest Payable	2,900
Inventory	31,000	Taxes Payable	6,100
Supplies	3,800	Warranty Liability	1,100
Prepaid Insurance	1,500	Unearned Revenues	1,500
Total Current Assets	89,000	Total Current Liabilities	61,000
Investments	36,000	**Long-term Liabilities**	
		Notes Payable	20,000
Property, Plant & Equipment		Bonds Payable	400,000
Land	5,500	Total Long-term Liabilities	420,000
Land Improvements	6,500		
Buildings	180,000		
Equipment	201,000	**Total Liabilities**	481,000
Less: Accum Depreciation	(56,000)		
Prop, Plant & Equip - net	337,000		
Intangible Assets		**STOCKHOLDERS' EQUITY**	
Goodwill	105,000	Common Stock	110,000
Trade Names	200,000	Retained Earnings	229,000
Total Intangible Assets	305,000	Less: Treasury Stock	(50,000)
		Total Stockholders' Equity	289,000
Other Assets	3,000		
Total Assets	$770,000	**Total Liab. & Stockholders' Equity**	$770,000

Appendix E - Income Statement

Income Statement For Month Ended June 30, 2010		
Revenues		
Net sales		$5,000.00
Rental revenue		1,000.00
Total revenues		$6,000.00
Expenses		
Wages expense	$1,500.00	
Cost of goods sold	1,000.00	
Utilities expense	250.00	
Supplies expense	250.00	
Total operating expenses		3,000.00
Net income/loss		$3,000.00

Appendix F - Cash Flow Statement

Cash Flows From Operating Activities:		
Net income		$34,000
Adjustments to reconcile net income to net cash provided by operating activities:		
Increase in accounts receivable	$(36,000)	
Increase in accounts payable	$ 5,000	
Net cash provided by operating activities		($31,000)
Cash Flows From Financing Activities:		$ 3,000
Issuance of common stock	$60,000	
Payment of cash dividend	$(14,000)	
Net cash provided by financing activities		
Net increase in cash		$46,000
Cash, January 1, 2003		49,000
Cash, December 31, 2003		-0-
		$49,000

Appendix G – Principal Financial Ratios

Financial Ratio	Formula	Measurements
Return on Total Assets	Operating Profit Before Income Tax + Interest Expense÷Average Total Assets	Measures rate of return earned through operating total assets provided by both creditors and owners
Return on Ordinary Shareholder's Equity	Operating Profit & Extraordinary Items After Income Tax – Preference Dividends÷Average Ordinary Shareholders' Equity	Measures rate of return earned on assets provided by owners
Gross Profit Margin	Gross Profit÷Net Sales	Measures the profitability of trading and mark-up
Profit Margin	Operating Profit after Income Tax÷Net Sales Revenue	Measures net profitability of each dollar of sales

Profitability Ratios

Asset Management Ratios

Financial Ratio	Formula	Measurements
Receivables Turnover	Net Sales Revenue÷Average Receivables	Measures the effectiveness of collections; used to evaluate whether receivables balance is excessive
Average Collection Period	Average Receivables Balance x 365÷Net Sales Revenue	Measures the average number of days taken by an entity to collect its receivables
Inventory Turnover	Cost of Goods Sold÷Average Inventory Balance	Indicates the liquidity of inventory. Measures the number of times inventory is sold on the average during the period
Total Asset Turnover	Net Sales Revenue÷Average Total Assets	Measures the effectiveness of an entity in using its assets during the period
Turnover of Fixed Assets	Net Sales÷Fixed Assets	Measures the efficiency of the usage of fixed assets in generating sales

Appendix H – Market Based Financial Ratios

Financial Ratio	Formula	Measurements
Earnings per share	Operating profits after income tax less Preference dividends ÷ Weighted average number of ordinary shares issued	Measures profit earned on each ordinary share.
Price-earnings ratio	Market price per ordinary share ÷ Earnings per ordinary share	Measures the amount investors are paying for a dollar of earnings.
Earning Yield	Earnings per ordinary share ÷ Market price per ordinary share	Measures the return to an investor purchasing shares at the current market price.
Dividend Yield	Annual dividend per ordinary share ÷ Market price per ordinary share	Measures the rate of return to shareholders based on current market price.
Dividend Payout	Total dividend per ordinary share ÷ Market price per ordinary share	Measures the percentage of profits paid out to ordinary shareholders.
Net Asset Backing	Ordinary shareholder's equity ÷ No. of ordinary shares.	Measures the assets backing per share.

Appendix I – Nothing In Between, LLC

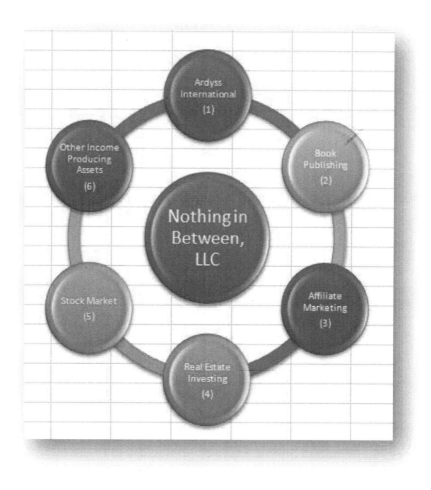